Old CRIEFF

by
Alex F. Young

A view from Monzie Camp, at the settlement of Monzie to the north of Crieff, which appeared on a postcard postmarked 28 July 1913. As they swung their picks and shovels, little could these men of the Black Watch have realised how much of their future would be spent in trenches – or of their horror. The fourth panel of the Crieff war memorial is devoted to the Black Watch and holds the names of one captain, two lieutenants, three sergeants, three corporals, eight lance corporals, two pipers and forty-six privates.

First published in the United Kingdom, 2003,
by Stenlake Publishing,
Telephone / Fax: 01290 551122

ISBN 1 84033 262 X

The publishers regret that they cannot supply copies of any pictures featured in this book.

ACKNOWLEDGEMENTS

The author wishes to thank David Campbell, Brian and Morag Campbell, David R. Cowan, Frank Thomson, Norman Adams, Elizabeth McIntyre, David and Jess Smith, William Tracey, Alex Douglas, The *Strathearn Herald*, Crieff Hydro Ltd, Crieff Golf Club, Susan Payne of Perth Museum, Pat Styles of the Scout Association, Gillian Lonergan of the Co-operative College, Manchester, Thos B. Smyth, archivist of the Black Watch, Jan Merchant and Steve Connolly of the A.K. Bell Library, Perth.

The publishers wish to thank Hugh and Jessie McArthur for contributing most of the photographs in this book from their collection. Thanks also to David Campbell for permission to reproduce the pictures on pages 10, 12 and 39, and David R. Cowan for those on pages 7 and 47.

FURTHER READING

The books listed below were used by the author during his research. None of them are available from Stenlake Publishing Ltd. Those interested in finding out more are advised to contact their local bookshop or reference library.

Handbook of the Forty-Fifth Annual Co-operative Congress, Aberdeen, Whitsuntide, 1913.
John Freeman, *Crieff Golf Club, 1891–1991*, 1991.
Francis H. Groome, *Ordnance Gazetteer of Scotland*, Thos C. Jack, London, 1885.
Nick Haynes, *Perth & Kinross: An Illustrated Architectural Guide*, The Rutland Press, 2000.
Rev. Charles M. Hepburn, *The Third Statistical Account, The Parish of Crieff*, 1951.
Rev. Alexander Laing, *The New Statistical Account, Parish of Crieff*, 1838.
Alexander Porteous, *The History of Crieff*, Oliphant, Anderson & Ferrier, Edinburgh & London, 1912.
Brian Wilton, *The Hydro of Yesteryear*, Crieff Hydro Hotel, 1993.

INTRODUCTION

The name Crieff derives from either *craobh* – 'among the trees' – or *crubha* – 'haunch or side of the hill', both of which refer to its position on the wooded hillside on the left bank of the River Earn. By 1218 it was a burgh of barony, capital of Strathearn, and the seat of civil and criminal jurisdiction. This 'heritable' right of the 'Lord of the Manor' to pit and gallows was repealed in 1748.

The town may be the 'Gateway to the Highlands', but this accident of geography, being neither lowland nor highland, has brought losses and gains. It was burnt by Jacobite Highlanders under John Erskine, Earl of Mar, on their retreat from the Battle of Sheriffmuir in November 1715 – but by a decade later, up to 30,000 black cattle from the north were passing through Crieff's October market on their way to England. In 1770 this market or 'tryst' moved to Falkirk.

Unlike the Rebellion of 1715, the '45 Rebellion left Crieff unscathed, despite the Drummond Arms having hosted the Pretender's last council of war. The Drummond family, who supported the Jacobites, faired less well and had to forfeit their estate to the crown until 1784.

The early 1730s saw the development of the town centre and the area around James Square under the hand of James Drummond, the third Duke of Perth. He also nurtured the beginnings of industrialisation with the introduction of flax, which led to a cottage industry in cotton weaving. The yarn was brought from Glasgow and the finished garments returned to the market there. In 1770 the weavers followed the national trend and formed themselves into a society which built the Weaver's Hall in Commissioner Street in 1786. By 1830 the town's 360 looms were producing 5,200 webs of cotton, each of 100 yards length. The population too was increasing. Webster's census of 1755 shows it as being 1,414, which by the 1830s had increased to 4,700.

The other main industry was farming which husbanded not only the finest cattle but also grain for brewing and distilling. By 1748 there were five breweries, and in 1775 Glenturret Distillery opened.

The nineteenth century was one of rapid change and improvement, with mains gas becoming available from 1842, and a water supply from Loch Turret in 1872. Previously, water was obtained from springs, principally that at Cold Wells (hence Coldwells Road). Electricity was introduced at an Electrical Exhibition in June 1920. The coming of the railway in 1856 meant easy access from most other places in the country.

In 1863 the burgh boundaries were set and a board of Commissioners established the following year. This again changed with the Burgh (Police) Scotland Act, 1892, and the town's management came under a council consisting of a provost, two bailies and nine councillors, with departments under the charge of the Town Clerk, Town Chamberlain, Burgh Surveyor, Sanitary Inspector, Housing Factor and Burgh Prosecutor.

The later nineteenth century brought Morrison's Academy and the 'Hydro', which, although neither were great sources of employment, brought both prestige and economic spin-offs. Changes in working conditions throughout the country introduced the concept of the family holiday and, with its more than adequate rail links, Crieff became a popular centre. This brought not only an increasing number of hotels, but also many rooms 'to let'.

Much has been written of the visit by Robert Burns to Ochtertyre in 1787, but the poet wrote only of the wild life on Loch Turret. It was left to the Dundonian, William McGonagall, to pen the immortal words: 'Ye lovers of the picturesque, if ye wish to drown your grief,/ Take my advice, and visit the ancient town of Crieff.'

Opposite: When Crieff's Tolbooth, built in 1685, was demolished around 1842 to make way for the present town hall, these seventeenth century stocks were found in one of the two basement cells. The few stocks used in Scottish towns were wooden (Stirling, Stonehaven, Edinburgh, Kinghorn, Kelso and one or two others had them), but this set were of wrought iron. This photograph from 1909 shows the surviving half of the device, which would have held four miscreants, when it was displayed outside the town hall. It is not known where it was sited when it was actually in use. The early Tolbooth records survived until 1798 when the Sutherland Fencibles, who were quartered in the Tolbooth, used them as kindling, but tradition tells that the stocks were last used in 1816, when Neil Young was the town officer, although neither the miscreant's name nor his offence is known. In his book *The History of Crieff*, Alexander Porteous wrote of the interest they generated at the Glasgow Exhibition of 1888 and lamented that at the time of writing they were rusting and corroding outside the town hall. He would be satisfied that they now form part of an indoor exhibition at the Town Hall.

The Murray Fountain and James Square, leading to Bank Place and King Street, in the early twentieth century. The North of Scotland Bank is now the offices of Perth and Kinross Council. Founded in Aberdeen in 1836, this bank merged with the Town and County Bank of Aberdeen in 1907 and was taken over by the Midland Bank in 1923. As Midland also owned the Clydesdale Bank, another merger created the Clydesdale and North of Scotland Bank in 1950 – 'North of Scotland' disappearing from the name in 1960.

Provost Frederick N. Hunt (1876–1948) reads the official proclamation of King Edward VIII from the steps of the Murray Fountain on Friday, 24 January 1936. In the foreground is the guard of honour, a detachment of members of the Officer Training Corps of Morrison's Academy. Throughout that week provosts up and down the country had braved the January weather, but little did they know then that they would be performing the task again in December. Following the abdication of King Edward VIII, Provost Hunt proclaimed the accession of King George VI from the steps of the North of Scotland Bank in James Square.

In the summer of 1929 sixteen year old Alexander 'Sandy' Smith cycles back through James Square to John Low, the poulterer's shop in West High Street, where he was apprentice-cum-message boy. He spent his Second World War service at Inveraray and worked for many years at Almondbank Naval Stores. Following his death in November 1989, his ashes were scattered on Conachon Hill.

James Square in February 1967 with at least two small boys appreciating an overnight fall of the snow. However, the road from Perth was open if the van from Frew's Garage got through.

With the Second World War over, the summer of 1946 brought holidaymakers back to Crieff, and the giant draughts board in James Square back into service. But who is winning?

The south side of High Street in the late 1930s or early '40s. Now forgotten by today's generation, the shops at that time included those of Speedie the chemist, Henderson the fishmonger, the milliner London House, Cooper the grocer, the saddler Cook, Bain's toy shop and Aitken the ironmonger. Beyond the Town Hall was the Dundee Equitable Boot Co. and Peter Crerar's Motor Tours.

From its foundation in 1875, Crieff and District Co-operative Society had struggled to survive – that is, until the opening of its new premises at 28 East High Street in 1912. From that point it had a membership of 218 from the town's population of 5,571, a turnover of £4,601 and paid a dividend of 2/-. This photograph, taken the following year, shows William Forsyth, manager (third from the right), McKenzie the baker (second from the left) and David Campbell, centre front.

Staff of the Strathearn Laundry at their premises on the corner of Ramsay Street on Leadenflower in the early 1900s. The gentleman on the right may be the laundry's founder, Mr Laing. When it was bought over in 1903 and became a limited company with John Crerar as secretary, one innovation was the introduction of 'French' or dry cleaning. The pervading smell of carbon tetrachloride, the cleaning agent, is one vivid memory of the area.

Drummond the plumber's premises at No. 16 East High Street, decorated for the coronation of King George V in June 1911. As was the case across the country, shops throughout Crieff were similarly bedecked with garlands and ribbons. Drummond's business would see two more coronations before closing in the late 1980s.

The High Street in 1948. On the right, past the junction with Hill Street is the Drummond Arms Hotel. This stands on the site of the original Drummond of Perth's Arms Inn, Tavern and Hotel, where the Pretender, Charles Edward Stewart, held a council of war on 3 February 1746.

A photograph contemporary with the previous view, but taken early enough in the morning to have caught Lipton the grocer taking a fruit and vegetable delivery and local men making their way to work at their offices or shops.

The north side of High Street around 1937, with the premises of Elliot the draper, Lipton the grocer (currently Oxfam), and Anderson the chemist. In April 1947 the latter was taken over by the Nottingham based chain, Boots the Chemist. Boots later moved across the street to their current location, taking over part of Thomson the ironmonger's shop.

Dominating Comrie Street, as it curves towards West High Street, is the Scoto–Gothic style red sandstone Free Church with its 120 feet tower. It was built between 1880 and 1882, at a cost of £4,500, by the Glasgow architect John J. Stevenson (1831–1908). Photographed in the summer of 1913, Crieff's already vigorous tourist industry is shown by the provision of afternoon teas, jellies and ices at Miss Norah Gordon's restaurant on the right. Running on from there are the premises of Miss G. Lynch the stationer, displaying newspapers and postcards, Donald McOmish the fruiterer, John Miller the grocer and J. Ford Balfour, another stationer. Due to dwindling numbers, the 860 seat church closed, becoming the Crieff Antique Centre in July 2000.

The committee formed to raise Crieff's memorial to the 167 men and two women of the district who gave their lives in the First World War commissioned the Glasgow architect Peter McGregor Chalmers (1859–1922) to design it and the Crieff builder, Peter Crerar, to erect it. Standing on its triangular plot on Burrell Street to a height of 24 feet and 6 inches, the memorial is a 'mercat cross' set on an octagonal basement which holds the cast bronze plates with the names of the fallen. The unveiling took place on a wet and windy Sunday, 20 November 1921, and was carried out by Major-General Sir Richard Bannatine Allason (1855–1940), after a march through the town headed by the pipers of the 6th Black Watch from Perth. The memorial's designer, Peter Chalmers, did not attend through ill-health and he died the following March. The two women commemorated, Jessie Elizabeth McRobbie and Mary Watson, were staff sisters with Queen Alexandra's Imperial Military Nursing Service. Staff Nurse Watson died on Wednesday 6 November 1918 and Staff Nurse McRobbie the following day; both were buried at Crieff. The Second World War added the names of forty-nine men and two women and the Malaya Conflict two more. The last name to be added was that of Lance Corporal Derek Duncan Blair of the Black Watch who was killed in Korea.

An early twentieth century photograph of Balmenoch House on Comrie Street, taken when Mr and Mrs Murphy ran it as the Grampian Hills Hydropathic. They advertised that their 'Successful Methods – Invigorating Baths, Packs, Fomentations, Sprays, Massage etc. – are the simple means used to aid the natural functions.' Obviously, the therapeutic effects of grass cutting were also recognised!

On his death in 1826, Thomas Morrison, a master builder in Edinburgh's New Town (where Morrison Street is named after him), left £20,000 in his estate and instructions for his trustees to 'erect and endow an institution . . . to promote the interests of mankind, having a particular regard to the Education of Youth'. This was to be in the Muthill area where he had been born. It took the trustees thirty-one years to find a site, the ten acre Market Park, and a further two years before the architects, Peddie & Kinnear of Edinburgh, had completed plans. The Scottish baronial style building – Morrison's Academy – was finally opened in October 1860.

In February 1867 the Strathearn Hydropathic Establishment Company Limited (later the Strathearn Sanatorium Company) issued a prospectus seeking £21,000 in 840 shares of £25 each, engaged Dr Thomas H. Meikle of the Loch-Head Hydropathic, Aberdeen, and chose the Knock of Crieff for its site. This view was taken in 1930.

In the pursuit of healthy, vigorous, exercise, tennis proved so popular at 'the Hydro' that the courts seen in this 1898 photograph displaced plans for a bowling green.

The feasibility of adding a winter garden to the hotel's facilities was discussed by the directors in 1900, but as the final plan included a ground level swimming pool, ten additional bedrooms and the winter garden on top, the work did not start until the spring of 1903. It was opened for Easter 1904, with the swimming pool opening the following year. Decked with palms and furnished in cane, the Winter Gardens proved a popular 'afternoon tea' venue, with the hotel orchestra enhancing the lively social atmosphere.

Crieff Bowling Club, on the corner of Victoria Terrace and Coldwells Road, around 1905. Founded in February 1867, the club was initially based at Mungall Park, beyond Turret Bridge, until its inconvenience was recognized and this site at Knock's Acre was leased from Drummond Estate at £2 per annum. Opened on 7 June 1890, the venture, including the pavilion (still used as a locker room) and the 42 yard square green of Ayrshire turf, cost around £600. In 1924 the club bought up the land for £100 and a new clubhouse was opened in 1967.

The Crieff Comedy Company in costume for *Doctor's Patients*, which, along with *Chiselling* and *Withered Leaves*, they presented in 1908. The Crieff Dramatic Club was started in 1884 by Mr Robert McKenzie, with *Rob Roy*, *The Spanking Legacy* and *Oor Geordie* in their repertoire. There was also Mr W.S. Douglas's burlesque version of *The Lady of the Lake*. Interest waned, but rose again in 1897 when Crieff Dramatic Society presented *The Lady of Lyons* and, ironically, *Rip Van Winkle*. These were the society's only shows, but theatre in Crieff slept only ten years before the Comedy Company was treading the boards in 1908. The money raised from these productions was gifted to the Cottage Hospital.

Formed in 1924 as a first class juvenile club and playing at Market Park, Earngrove Football Club, in their blue and white hooped tops, joined the Perth and District Junior League in 1935–36, when they finished runners-up with this team. *Back row, left to right*: E. Hayes (asst trainer), J. Anderson, Jimmy Graham from Braco, John Ross, Peter Welsh (goalkeeper), Davie Leckie, Donald Blyth, bootmaker and saddler, and Ben Wright. *Front row*: George Glashan, who restarted the club after the war, A. Munro, Jimmy Reid (Capt.), G. Simpson, Robert 'Tiger' McGraw, and Ben Wright Junior, the 'Mascot' in front. One of the best remembered stories about the club comes from the Second World War, when, with so many men in the forces, football was all but abandoned (Peter Welsh, Earngrove's goalkeeper, spent part of his war as a POW). Meeting Jeanfield Swifts in the Perthshire Cup, Earngrove were beaten 13–1 – a drubbing – and were to meet them again the following week in the Scottish Cup. Midweek, Manager Sandy Jamieson called at the requisitioned 'Hydro' and 'signed' six men of the HLI and five from the Black Watch to take the field against the Swifts. The result – a 1–0 victory for Earngrove! The team re-formed in 1945 and played until the 1960s. There was a break and then the team continued until the mid 1970s.

Following their inaugural meeting on 27 May 1890, Crieff Golf Club invited the legendary 'Old Tom' Morris of St Andrews Golf Course to select the best of the potential sites and lay out a nine hole course. Opting for East Ledbowie Park, the work was completed for the opening on 11 July 1891, when the Earl of Winchelsea drove off the first ball on the 2,385 yard course. Two years later the club moved to Culcrieff, but this too was a nine hole course and the increasing demand for an eighteen hole course forced the move to Ferntower in 1914. Two years later this, their new clubhouse, designed by local architect William Finlayson, was completed. It was replaced in 1990.

A view of King Street, running to James Square, taken from the entrance to the railway station in the summer of 1906. Beyond the bridge over the railway line to Comrie is the Victoria Temperance Hotel.

Crieff Railway Station with King Street beyond, 1908. The railway came to Crieff in 1856, when the Crieff Junction Railway opened the line to Gleneagles. Ten years later the Perth, Almond Valley & Methven Railway opened their line from Perth and in 1893 extended it to Comrie. The centre line allowed goods trains to pass unimpeded.

A Dunalastair class engine, originally built for the Caledonian Railway, photographed in the livery of the London Midland Scottish at Crieff Station in 1935. At this time the station was handling upwards of fifty trains per day, but by the late 1950s passenger numbers were so reduced that a diesel railbus, on a less frequent service, was introduced. This merely delayed the inevitable and the station closed in July 1964.

It is 1909. It is Crieff Railway Station. And this group of fifty-one men, and a boy, are heading home having won the Cup. But for what? Some are too old for football, while others are too young for bowls!

No civic event would have been complete without the town band, pictured here at the beginning of the twentieth century. The style of uniform, with bandolier, would suggest military roots, but sadly no record of its members has survived. Predecessors of this band are said to have played at the cutting of the first turf for the Crieff Junction Railway in 1854.

Crieff's Philharmonic Society was founded in 1850. This photograph of its members was taken by McKenzie of Ferntower Road Studio in 1907. None of the musicians can be named although the violinist, seated front centre, may be Dr Turner. Their connection with Crieff Operatic Society would have ensured a repertoire embracing the works of Gilbert and Sullivan.

Stretching between Strowan Road and the River Earn, this area was a flood plain until its use as a municipal dump raised it to a safe level. Around 1948 the town council grassed it over and made it into a camp site, shown in this 1955 photograph. The position of the present Braidhaugh Caravan Park is out of picture to the right.

Originally a keep, the locally quarried brown sandstone built Drummond Castle dates from 1491 when King James IV granted the lands to John, First Lord Drummond. King James IV was gifted cherries from the garden during a hunting trip to Glen Artney Forest in 1508. The early seventeenth century saw the beginnings of the garden's formal Italian style layout and the Mylne sundial dates from 1630. Queen Victoria and Prince Albert visited in 1842 and, according to the Queen, they 'walked in the garden which is really very fine, with terraces, like an old French garden'.

The piper of Drummond Castle standing by the portcullis entrance in 1907. Employed as a factotum, piping would have been one his many duties. He cannot be named but, being a left handed player, it has been suggested he was a Highlander.

One of the photographs taken between 17 and 18 August 1906 to mark the visit to Drummond Castle of King Alphonso XIII and Queen Ena of Spain. The King (centre) spent his time on the grouse moor and was the party's best shot. Born in 1886, he was the posthumous son and successor to Alphonso XII, with his mother, Maria Christina, being regent until 1902. In 1906 he married Princess Victoria Eugenie of Battenburg, a granddaughter of Queen Victoria. Following the First World War, in which Spain did not participate, the country drifted to republicanism and in April 1931 Alphonso went into exile. He died in 1941.

The first Crieff Highland Games were held in the grounds of Morrison's Academy in 1870 when the Chieftain was Captain Henry E.H. Drummond Moray Junior of Abercairney. The move to Market Park came in 1880 as the tramp of thousands of feet was damaging the school's cricket pitch. In 1890 a permanent grandstand was built and by 1924, with additions and improvements, could seat 950. This photograph shows the festooned and garlanded stand at the 1904 games. On 11 October 1973 it was destroyed by fire.

Expecting to see King Alphonso of Spain, a record crowd of 12,000 attended the Crieff Games in 1906. However, they were to be disappointed as the attraction of Drummond Castle's grouse moors was too strong for the King. The piper in the photograph cannot be identified, but so engrossed are the judges that he is clearly the class winner!

Lord Sumers, Deputy Chief Scout, takes the salute at the march past of 3,500 Scouts, from forty-two countries, at the opening of the Third World Rover Scout Moot at Monzie Castle, 15–26 July 1939. As an international event, it was broadcast by the BBC, as was the closing ceremony at Murrayfield Rugby Ground, Edinburgh. The first Rover Scout Moot had been at Kandersteg, Switzerland, in 1931, but with the Second World War only weeks away, this would be the last until 1949, when Skjak in Norway played host.

The Scout Movement had expected 8,000 Rover Scouts, but events in Europe discouraged many from sending contingents, although, ironically, there was one from Poland, which would be invaded six weeks later. This photograph shows one of the many kitchens, but it was not all work. There were international football matches: Scotland v. England, Edinburgh v. London, and 'Glasgow's challenge to the world'. A Moot XV played Crieff at rugby and won, and Perthshire at cricket and lost. Organised expeditions climbed Ben Vorlich, Ben Lawers and Ben Nevis, while sailors and fishermen headed for Loch Earn, Loch Leven and Loch Turret.

During the Moot, early each morning the Laird of Monzie's piper, John McGregor, played from the castle turret as the flag was unfurled and piped the flag party back to the camp. McGregor's reveille was not fully appreciated by all, and here he says farewell to his *alter ego*, who was thereafter laid peacefully to rest.

This 1940s view of Macrosty Park illustrates the ongoing improvements the council made to the park, with the provision of swings and a pool in the children's area. A native of Crieff and three times provost of the town, James Macrosty (born 1824) gifted this park to the town in 1902 and although he was at the opening ceremony, on 9 August, the coronation day of King Edward VII, he was too ill to participate, leaving the ceremonials to his grandson, James Macrosty. He died in June 1906.

Added within a year or two of the park's opening, the bandstand became a focal point on summer's afternoons and evenings. Although the railing around it is gone, the bandstand has come through the twentieth century remarkably well.

The park's putting green, tennis courts and tearoom in 1950. Today there are fewer bicycles – but a larger car park.

A group of men of the Black Watch pose for the photographer at Monzie Camp in July 1912.

Pipers of the 6th Black Watch (Royal Highlanders) on parade at Monzie Camp in 1912. One of the two pipers named on the war memorial at Crieff is Alexander Keddie, who served with this battalion.

E Company of the 6th Black Watch on the march from Monzie Camp in July 1914. This Perthshire Territorial battalion of the regiment spent the first months of the First World War at Queensferry, defending the Forth Bridge under the command of Captain W. Alexander. They were posted to Flanders, France, in May 1915 where they remained for the duration of the war. For assisting the French Army at the Battle of Tardenois, 20–30 July 1918, the regiment was awarded the Crois de Guerre.

An early twentieth century fisherman and his family in the lea of the Burns Rock on the west bank of Loch Turret. On the opposite bank is Turret Lodge and its ancillary buildings. The rock commemorates the visit of Robert Burns to Loch Turret in 1787. Having walked from Ochtertyre House, where he was a guest of Sir William Murray, he found the inspiration for the poem 'On Scaring Some Water-Fowl In Loch Turit'. The opening lines – 'Why, ye tenants of the lake,/ For me your wa'try haunt forsake?/ Tell me, fellow-creatures, why/ At my presence thus you fly?' – contradict the claim that Burns was wildfowling. The Rock and the Turret Lodge were lost when the building of Loch Turret Dam in 1963–68 raised the water level 20 feet and lengthened the loch from 1 mile to 2 miles.

Crieff had secured its water supply from Loch Turret in 1872, but with increasing demands from consumers across the east central belt as far as Grangemouth, Balfour, Beatty & Lilley started the five year project on the new Loch Turret Dam in 1963. This new reservoir's surface was 180 feet above sea level, increased the loch's length to 2 miles and its depth (when full) to 90 feet. It supplies 18.5 million gallons of water to 200,000 consumers.

Pittentean Crossing, south of Crieff, in the aftermath of extensive flooding across Perthshire, following a freak succession of blizzard snow, rapid thaw and torrential rain (two and half inches in twenty-four hours) in January 1909. Here, only the road was lost, but a number of lives were lost and flocks of sheep swept away. Standing on the roadway is William Wishart the level crossing keeper.